ELEMENTS OF LIFE

A living series…

notionpress.com

ELEMENTS OF LIFE

A living series...

Inderjit Kaur

notionpress.com

Notion Press

5 Muthu Kalathy Street, Triplicane,

Chennai - 600 005

First Published by Notion Press 2014

ISBN: 978-93-84391-68-3

Dedicated...

This book is dedicated to my father,

Late Shri Jaswant Singh Hira

At times it was difficult and you seeded the thought of believing in yourself and the power of will that can change all the difficult times into peace. I now see the perfection and meaning of my life in every moment.

I love you, Dad....

THOUGHT

"And, when you can't go back, you have to worry only about the best way of moving forward."

- Paulo Coelho, The Alchemist

INTRODUCTION

Air –Adjust – Live Purely like the Air.
Water –Adapt – Flow Courageously like Water.
Fire – Acquire – Glow Compassionately like Fire.
Earth –Accept – Move gratefully like Earth.

Life is a blend of Trials and Errors.

Try all possibilities re-focus all probabilities that life offers you - and face what is to be faced on the way.

Accept, adapt, refocus and reinvent. Work hard, but make it look easy.

A bird must learn to walk before it can fly. So we must recollect all the broken pieces of our souls and learn again, try again, as life is a process that takes time.

We expect happiness, but reality often presents difficulties. In anticipation of hardships, struggles and adapting to change, this book offers a treasure chest of 'never give up' mantras.

Elements of Life explores the options and choices which will help you to work on the best path for you to lead a full and harmonious life. To live more in tune with what you want out of life. Motivational chapters relating to simple questions based on the elements of life - air, fire, water and earth - provide strategies in the form of pearls of wisdom.

This book will assist you in clearing your emotional clutter. It will physically, mentally and spiritually retrieve, restore and revive your trust in life.

Elements of Life is presented in sections for the reader's ease of understanding.

Study: is presented in four sections relating to the elements of life - air, water, fire and earth – each section awakens the reader to a journey of self-discovery with the goal of keeping the balance of mind and body.

Read the special pearls of wisdom at the conclusion of each section. Find the resemblance to life in the specific elements at the end of each chapter.

My Journal: is in two sections which express my goals... "Say, Yes to Life" and "Yes, I Can."

My Journal is a simple tool with positive affirmation quotes for readers, designed to help you thrive during times of change. Motivational material to bring enthusiasm back into your life.

Simple tools providing the solutions that you were looking for to make your life awesome once again.

Elements of Life is a guide book to bring the reader back to a positive state of mind, thus creating a more meaningful and rich life experience.

Foreword

Inderjit Kaur is a remarkable person. If you know anything about her personal life and journey you'll be as amazed as I am about her positive attitude and her inspirational writing. Her first book '***Living a More Meaningful Life***' astonished me with its simple and enlightening snippets of wisdom. She has done it again with this gem and I am delighted and honoured to introduce you to yet another wonderful book by this gifted author. Her messages speak to me and should do to everyone: "Say Yes to Life!", "Say Yes I Can!" and "Shine!" - commands we all have heard, we all know are important for our happiness and still, we so often forget about them, causing our own misery. What I love about this book in particular is the inclusion of the four elements: Air, Water, Earth and Fire. Using them and the associated analogies goes back to Ancient Astrology and they have filled human imagination from the beginning of speech. They all have their unique powers and strengths - they connect us to Nature and to a simpler way of living and thinking. Included in this book are also more Pearls of Wisdom and a Journal Part. I invite you to enjoy the gift that is ***Inderjit Kaur*** and the gift that is her body of work.

Christoph Fischer- Author of the historical 'Three Nations Trilogy', comprising of 'The Luck oftheWeissensteiners' Slovakia, WW2), 'Sebastian' (Vienna, WW1) and 'The Black Eagle Inn' (Germany, post WW2). Also author of 'Time to Let Go', a contemporary family drama about Alzheimers' Disease, and 'Conditions', a contemporary family drama about mental health and friendship.

- Christoph Fischer

Author's Note

Of course, everyone wants to live in peace and happiness at the end of the day. We all need an environment filled with peace and happiness, where we can live life in true meaning.

Where we can live in patience, act calmly in peaceful living and compassionate ways.

Elements of life is revolutionized and embedded with all these simple, peaceful pearls relevant for a meaningful life. If we are feeling low, if we are uninspired, we are finding it hard to cope with the stress of life, and if we do not change - we may be on the edge of extinction. We may lose our precious life without living in it.

Elements of Life *is one of the pearls from the -* ***living series.***

Living a more meaningful life is a debut in the series *so, let us begin with a new day and with a new thought filled with positivity and enthusiasm..*

Inderjit Kaur

ACKNOWLEDGEMENTS

This book would have not existed without the kind support of my family and friends.

I sincerely thank you Arjun and Mandeep, my lovely sons for being enthusiastic throughout. You and your positive energy are astonishing.

I want to record the support, interest and encouragement shown by Simarjit, Theresa Synder, Paul Hollis, for assisting with all the positive words while drafting elements of Life and being my strength also I would like to thank Renuka Nair and Alpna for being supportive friends

Theresa Synder renowned scifi fantasy writer of 'The Farloft Chronicles' for encouraging and fuelling me with positive feeds at times and for being a wonderful friend always. Thank you Theresa for being so supportive at all times. Your kind words are always appreciated.

My deepest gratitude to my author friend Paul Hollis, the award-winning writer of the Hollow Man series, for assisting and feeding in valuable positive suggestions while drafting my work. Paul your kind efforts are much appreciated. I would also like to extend my gratitude to Advocate Edgar Percy Breganza and Advocate Edgar Kennedy Breganza (advocate, High Court, Mumbai). Thank you for encouraging me always, in all my difficult times and your continued kind support.

This book would not have been complete without the Foreword presented by able Author Christoph Fischer, the writer of class books like 'Three Nations Trilogy', 'Time to Let Go', and 'Conditions', a contemporary family drama about mental health and friendship.

And finally, the loving divine energy that flows through my life every single day, I am grateful always to:

Shirdi Sai for showing me the way to walk the right path of living....

I want to also acknowledge the publishing team at ***Notion Press***, all the people who had a hand in making this possible.

Contents

PART A - STUDY

I. Authentic Air

What really matters?

- ✦ Graph of Life legible
- ✦ Believe in the process called Life
- ✦ Life is now
- ✦ Life odysseys ~ panoply
- ✦ Life's lessons learned
- ✦ Simplicity ~ The essence of ecstasy
- ✦ Pearls of wisdom ~ Air

1. What Really Matters?

Keep Living - Adjusting like Air; balancing your life in all the areas from the home to the workplace, to relationships and towards life. No matter what life hurls at you, it is the way you respond, that matters.

If you don't change for the better you may land on the edge of extinction.

You can live in the past or long for a bright future. However, it does matter how much you can get involved in the setting up of your own self. Seize the moment. Start working towards your goals and just look ahead. What can be more challenging than to challenge yourself to improve?

Putting right things first, adhering to what you believe. Establishing consistency between what you think, what you mean, what you do, what you want... can provide a valid breakthrough in all the uncertainties of life.

If you're genuine and are not overburdened with unhappiness and dishonesty, the chances of facing the truth and getting a suitable solutions to your problems that will relay in the most positive manner and in terms of best possibilities will eventually occur, fading failures away. You got to keep flowing, authentic like air in all walks of life.

Happiness is a process. It's like a toolkit combined with various associated factors.

It's the concept you choose while being authentic that matters. Living fair, flowing like air in an acceptable, adaptable and accountable manner will ease your progress.

Keep Living Authentic like Air~

2. *Graph of LIFE ~ Legible*

Schema of 3C - Courage, Confidence, Commitment...

~ COURAGE is the Key

Every Element embedded in this unexplained life is in deliverance of a radiant opportunity and is submerged in the enlightenment of the inner self. Assorted thoughts infuse tremendous uncertainties, which may become subjective in concern. Life cannot seamlessly flow - there have to be curves of ups and downs. Sceptical sometimes, we forget to seek all the elements in reference to the graph of life, which when sublimated, emerges as a tiny dot of dust.

The moment you decide from your core that you will endure a little courage filled with convictions, you start overcoming the little uncertainties in your path very easily. Just how many times do we accept our flaws and try to rectify them? A very little courage is needed in to push for momentum and keep the event moving.

Why allow a single failure or a small setback to push back the momentum in your thoughts, encouraging you to give up?

Just drive closely inheritance to what you believe Nothing is impossible. Some storms of life damage all the paths and create uncertainties. But by reviving a little courage, you can still walk in that path, dare to find what was left behind. If the path is still difficult, just regain a little more of your courage, make a new path that is more convenient more vivid, pertaining you to get souvenirs at the reach. If you find yourself surrounded in darkness, just retrieve a little strength and bring in a thought that this situation is just like a caterpillar waiting in the dark for its colourful, vibrant wings to grow.

Waiting in the dark helps you build positivity, helping you gain inner strength, encouraging you with the most excellent perceptions of life - and teaches you patience. Courage and Patience are built subcutaneously - they need each other more often. Don't move a single step forward in the absence of both. This is the simplest strategy that works in times of turbulence, in the most devastating situations.

~ *CONFIDENCE the Ruler*

Limitations are encrypted only in our thoughts. We need to actively clear this lining of limitations, building in more confidence with affirmations. Once we are released from our limitations, we clear all the darker stumbling blocks of fears, the blocks of faded conceptions. We can now focus on our hidden potentials, investing in new opportunities that are relevant to realise our proposed dreams.

It's not the strongest or the most intelligent mind that survives the struggles and hardships of life. It is the mind that adapts, the process converting every moment into new opportunities, and that can conceive and re-design the great graph of success, that scales new heights.

Confidence wrapped in layers of ambition helps in this remarkable transition.
It's the act of courage and confidence in the present, that embeds the roots of Prosperity deeper and makes you stand encouraged and in affirmation, in the midst of storms.

Confidence makes you believe in the process now. Confidence makes you stand firm, manifesting your soul in pure positive elements, which in turn help you regain your enthusiasm and your radiance, making you overcome all fears, helping your inner self regenerate positively. You will emerge a more confident human being.

Confidence reconditions all the unbalanced barriers, elevating your purpose of living more significantly.

Confidence makes you reach the apex of your glory in radiance, in excellence.

~ COMMITMENTS

You have to fight through all your struggles and hardships to reach your success. You have to blend determination, self-belief, ambitions and devotion in affirmations to scale new heights.
Commitments proposed are needed to be perceived.

Being present in the process enhances your ability to develop, makes you concentrate more on the possibilities. It also enables you to shine in success, conquering your fears, thus making you grow from within.
Stay focused with all positive radiant energy.
Abundance of willpower and discipline can contribute fascinating performance.
Commitments proposed are needed to be considered as important, and are also needed to be conceived with in a given time frame.
Being disciplined in principles will make you feel gratified and help you set your goals redeemable into reality.

Immature thoughts make it difficult to pace with life thus your thoughts and your words that you commit are needed to be screened in affirmations. Stand positive to your commitments just do not give up if things get delayed

Allow these measures to set you on the path to Prosperity...Synchronize now your Courage, Confidence and Commitments ~And get the desired results.

Hence now ***the graph of life is legible,*** more efficient, more graceful in ambience of purposeful living.

3. *Believe in the Process called Life*

Seek the Truth ~

Those who Believe... find it

Let the Canvas of Life ultimately redeem more flamboyantly precisely in simplicity, in perfection, in harmony and in projections of serenity. Is this too much? No. Presumably every setback, every failure, unknowingly offers you chances to reinvent yourself as better disciplined and focused. It's actually giving you one more chance,offering you benefits from unattainable probabilities.

Just consider it a challenge. When you act in diligence, applying the simple strategies of patience and awareness, you redirect yourself at broadening your perspectives and are able to fly in wings which are coloured by brighter horizons.

Believe in the process. Believe in the purity of purposeful delays that seem extreme. You may find it hard to still accept unavoidable circumstances, but things will improve and your will surmount them with ease. Facing problems and failures as challenges, as responsibilities, you begin to grow. It's like a radiant new opportunity has been directed towards you, to help you replenish the hidden potential within,helping you attain what you deserve as the best.

The very fact which keeps the spirit enlightened is the desire to make a change,are the circumstantial challenges that area test for yourself.

The tougher the challenges, the better lessons inculcated.

You attain all the corresponding capacities consistent with the re-conditioning of your courage,helping you face more and more each day.

Every day, you see changes which are spontaneous. You begin to scale the highest levels of self-determination and self-belief. Now you take a major leap. You overcome your fear, you are now boundless, there are no limitations to your dreams, to your success, to your achievements.

Act in Strength and in patience while facing critical times.

At critical times, we feel very broken inside. Floating in failures and tormented in setbacks that aggregate various factors that trigger unnecessary agonies, these make us more deprived and depressed. Now this has to be attended to very carefully. You have to consistently project and redirect your mind to the present.

There is no other simple strategy to this. Just start living in the present. Leave behind the yesterday. Leave behind the darkest moments. Leave behind all that is gone.

Only those who seek may find the actual truth and that is the truth of the present moment.
If we try to re-energise this particular moment which is now very much with us, in radiance of hope, in directions of faith, we can still rule over the critical phase in more graceful ambience. Transform the crucial moment by just converting it into an opportunity. An opportunity to meet a new version of yourself who can cross the Road of Uncertainties, accepting the challenges. Try to write this down, highlighting what you wish to achieve .Write also what you wish to leave behind. Now you determine what fails and what wins.
Redirect yourself one more time. Regaining all your strength, just wipe out all the negative factors around you.

It's not so hard. Just a little more effort is needed here. Dedicate yourself to getting transformed into a positive energy. Act in strength while facing critical times. Acquiring the same positive approach now, move step-by-step ahead, in affirmations. See the

Immensely Powered Positivity inculcated by you for you, work for you.

Changes are spontaneous. Changes are important part of life accept adapt them with more of your courage. Changes are for better growth of your life when you accept a change in positivity this makes a possible start to a new beginning. A new horizon can be explored in success, in radiance, in peace, in persistence and all your fears get transformed into a new opportunity and you begin to rise above the problems and fly in success with no limits being imposed on you. You start to believe more in yourself, delving into your inner growth, searching the truth for self-awareness. Enlightened from within, you try to convert each problem into an opportunity that indirectly helps you to grow. This indirectly helps you in determining your own self-awareness, which leads to positively enhanced growth.

Translate every event, every conjunction, into the essence of empowerment.

4. Life is now in this Moment

As I begin to write, it's exactly 4.30 in the morning - my favourite time of the day. I still have an hour more to go for my routine chaos of work to take over. It's absolutely silent outside and I'm complete solitude.

There's something rejuvenating and peaceful about being alone and having some time to reflect, work or simply enjoy the silence.

More recently, I've learned to live in the present moment. To be privileged to be in this serene life, is akin to living your entire life in one moment. More precisely, I would emphasize that the so-called 'living', is just existing. Peace of mind is when we are able to live in the present moment more focused, more in enthusiasm,

irrespective of what happened yesterday or what may happen in the future. The present moment is where we stay all the time.

Sensing fascinations and eagerness life is actually being mastered and spend without a doubt more in worries deeply in the things that may never happen. We ourselves allow our past problems and future concerns to dominate our present moments - so much so that we are in frustration, depression and find ourselves vulnerable to starting to lose hope. On the other hand, we also postpone our gratification, our priorities and our happiness, often convincing ourselves that 'Someday' will be better than today. Unfortunately, we recommend ourselves to let go of the present moment without actually living in it.

`*Life is what is happening now*`

While we are busy making other plans, we forget to see that the people around us those who love us are moving away; our lives getting shorter, our bodies are getting physically, mentally and spiritually tired. Our dreams are slipping away - every second slips away without being lived in. Yes, we indeed miss out on life as if it was always there for us, very much for us.

Many people live as if they were in a dress rehearsal for some later date.
It isn't.
In fact, life treats us in love. We have to live in the life is still in us.
Now is the only time we that have with us - the present moment.

Fear for tomorrow is only a concern in our minds for the events that may or may not necessarily happen. So bring your attention back to the present moment and live a better life in enthusiasm and happiness.

Continuously direct your mind to live in present - you will always have boundless energy and you will start to live in enthusiasm.

5. Life's Odysseys or Panoply

Life ~ An Event

Life uncovers unexplained events sometimes.
We often accept the terms of life without trying to make any changes. We are like calm still pond water without flow. What does now happen?
Our inner being gets stagnant without any life.
Though we try to seek the world,our inner being is still not in peace.
Many questions still remained to be explored, explained.
Experiences of life reveal great lessons explaining every tiny resource - of how, when,why, did those things happen.
For everything, every happening there is a reason.
We have to accept that some reasons may be because of circumstantial challenges.
We have to find the very purpose being in the odysseys to the truth of life - what is the simplest way to get the desired dream fulfilled by closely seeking our inner instincts.

We got to shed the shackles of unreasonable thoughts and place a tremendous trust in our intuition.
When we release all our uncertainties all our unnecessarily coupled negativity, we are able to explore more of our inner centred self, the being which craves to live in balance of mind body soul. Revealed with great Emotions, we sometimes seek the attractive illusions outside our inner self. Since we are streaming in inner turmoil, we ignore the seeking of peace.
We start to destroy our own mind, body and soul in convictions that are temporary, passing, or false emotions.
We have to reinvent ourselves again.

~ Define

The events that we face in form of the challenges, in the form of our problems, in the form of our struggles, are to be looked upon as lessons.
Every event that happens, everything that happens, is for a lesson. Every setback engraves a lesson for us to learn from.
We have to realize, we have to define the very purpose of our failures. Whether the failures were professional, or subjected into emotional traumas or may be financial loss, all failures are essential. They in fact,helped us explore more of ourselves, our potential, and our inner abilities. It redefined us in the expansion to our inner limitations which could

never be explored otherwise.
It is only the failures that define you, inculcating the desires of great interest in seeking those golden keys of inner fulfillment, everlasting happiness and the urge for radiant health.
There is a tremendous difference in being well and being well off. So for the sake of living we pretend to ourselves that we are happy.
We unknowingly adapt unhappiness into a form of happiness, which when lost, breaks us and puts us in turmoil, in a crisis of pain.
Once we define our priorities, we can handle these temporary breakdowns and seek contentment. We can start cultivating a deep sense of inner peace, seeking serenity in the odysseys of our life.
We redirect our paths by being in peace, being in harmony, being in serenity of life - thus growing more energetic, living more joyfully, in spontaneity with the beauty of life.

~ Improve ~ Live Life

When we seek, we get the desired remedies coupled with sharp wisdom. Now we can integrate our instincts, redirecting ourselves.
Re-orienting our decision-making process towards enlightenment, we can move into a new horizon of serenity, radiating a more glorified destiny.
We keep on trading our whole life for the accumulation of materialistic fulfilment. All the potential we have, all our energy, is lost in the unnecessary illusions that we seek outside.

Once we start venturing out of our cocooned and self-constructed limitations, we find inner peace. We feel liberated from all the stress and strain of the odysseys of life. Constantly caring for ourselves, caring for our thought process, caring for our bodies, we feel personified from within as if the inner compass had nudged us and redirected us peacefully to our destination. Personal awakening and enlightenment from within is the actual zenith of success. Being successful outside is meaningless if we are not successful from within. If we cannot care for ourselves, how we can care for someone else?
Ultimately, the destiny unfolds according to what we choose in our lives.
We can choose to care for ourselves, and take the responsibility of being able to stand back while learning from our trials and our limitations. We can rise now from all that is weighing us down.
By developing a deep trust in life, we can now effectively improve our living, impacting our surroundings as well.

We can now thus

Seek ~ Define ~Redirect ~Explore ~Trust~ Live more, thanks to the enlightened odysseys of life and by not merely displaying temporary happiness and endorsing it as peaceful living.

So now make a choice

~ Life as an odyssey of happiness or panoply.....

6. Life ~Lessons Learned

The Collage of Vibrant Lessons
Enveloped As Experiences....

Life - A Euphoria of Joy Sometimes
Life - A Euphoria of Pains Sometimes

When applied correctly – Life is nothing but the balance of every event.
We tend to learn at every stage of life.

Lessons learned at various stages accumulated at one place is like a big jigsaw puzzle that collectively enhances into positive growth.
Some people may precisely learn from all the events, perhaps some wait to learn from personal experiences. Unknowingly enduring unnecessary pain, we tend to remain in a state of distress in the process of life.

Sensitive to such concerns, I would like to thus offer you the remedy that will help break the spell of uncertainties.

Most of the problems and challenges that are faced or will be faced in the course of a life have already been made. All the answers and all the solutions are thus inscribed onto some great pages of history.
Like we all know we are living in some of our inculcated habits. Those may be further channelled, as good or bad. The antidote to this is but within ourselves.
We can always step out of our cocooned lives and analyse the things that we are doing right and those that we are doing wrong.
There's nothing wrong in making mistakes.
In fact, mistakes are a part of life. They are essential for growth. In short, we can get to the heart of unsettled circumstances.

We can figure out how to make best use of time.
We can indeed find out more ways to curb the losses incurred.
What went wrong in our day? We can overcome failures by just re-examining what went wrong in Life.

We can revive the process of life by actually recognizing the areas that require improvements with immediate effect.
Rejuvenating the quality of life start living into life as yes life is indeed a gift indeed.
We can choose better ways inculcating radiant and peaceful living in our daily processes.
Lessons are to be mastered as self-learning teaching

aids. Regaining trust once again in Patience, Courage, Confidence, Commitment and Disciplines - the Collage of Vibrant Lessons can be Reconstructed, Revived Again.

Performance and reliability are the basic principles for a Successful Life. Courage allows us to do what we are seeking and since we know we have already conceived the thought, we are half done. Courage gives us self-control to perform constantly. Every element embedded has been directed so that you replenish the hidden potential. As you try a little more with passion and determination, you can overcome all the hurdles. You see that no challenge is too tough for you to surmount.

To break some of the habits which are curbing your growth, you just require a start. All it takes is 21 days to build the habits of life time.
Start with being an early riser.

As we know, an average person needs only six hours of peaceful sleep to restore the body and de-stress. The quality of sleep is essential, not the quantity. Rising with the sun makes you to start your day in positivity, in affirmations. To build the habit of being an early riser will be tiring initially. It will be also be difficult to install a new routine – it is like wearing a new shoe, which is at first hard, but after sometime, it becomes easy as soft as a feather with continued wear. Continuous efforts will provide the required results.

Rising early, taking a walk in the orange-gold sunlight can be a serene experience. It rejuvenates your inner self, restores your harmony with yourself, giving you peace.
Positive thoughts in the mornings can make your whole day more positive and productive.
The degree of your determination makes the purpose of living a more meaningful life, more possible.

Thus, learn to view all life's lessons as a collage – as a grandmaster may view them, making you aware of every move of life.

7. Simplicity, the Essence of Ecstasy

Being in Reception of Only Positive Elements...

The journey of LIFE is perhaps empirical. Simple living proposing great virtues in small proportions, leads to the opening of doorways in ambience of purposeful principles radiating the very purpose of life.
One day, quite simply, I thought to seek the very purpose of the profoundly-influenced, positively-fuelled happiness in each and every little event of life.

Enthralled to search all the possible enveloped strategies as I was Searching little lessons that fuelled me in making a constructive inbound repair forever. After great deliberations, I finally continued in the conviction that happiness is always there - we just need to define all the circumstances of our life and most importantly, interpret it and process it into the actual flow of what it actually means.

While experiencing this, I found that the chirpy notes of a sparrow could take me to the heights of happiness.
Just like the bells of a temple or a church, regenerate life around us in the form of sweet frequencies, soothing our desperate souls seeking peace.

Cultivating the seeds of gratitude makes a drastic Change...

While we consider all that we face either in negativity or in positivity
we should always be able to choose in informed wisdom,those that can be transferred into timeless principles for radiant living.
This sometimes feels frivolous or may even feel childish. But the more we analyse the self, the more we remind ourselves, the more we can be masters of our diamond-studded lives.

Being always in gratitude for every event that life has offered you, makes you shine in the richness that life offers.
Cultivating this great art - that of being in gratitude - makes an impact that many of us don't even realize...
The enormous positive attributes that we develop now is what which makes us strong emotionally and spiritually. Because now, most of the energy built inside our mind will help to strengthen us from within forever.

Take a little time to strengthen yourself through mere appreciation of special occasions that you find in the very vast events of life.

Life is a Gift -Live in Radiance- Live in Peace - Live in Patience; that is the only Key.

8. Pearls of Wisdom, Element Air

Balancing negative thoughts with more constructive ones keeps unwanted hassles away at critical times. Like Air, keep living – reasoning the facts: keeping cool.

Don't forget that sensitive expressions are vital for a fulfilling life. Balancing the negative feelings from high pressure zones, being patient, moving calmly towards low pressure zones... is like air that moves constantly. It keeps the mind-body-actions in perfect balance. Balancing all the impossible turns that hardships bring on your path and re-orienting yourself leads to

Building a strong confidence in the self. It encourages you and empowers you to deal with all unexpected, unexplained circumstances which were insurmountable, once more, strategically.

Explore what is needed.

Sometimes what you want may not be what you need.

One simple counterbalance is to explore the different aspects of your personality with the different conflicts of wants.

Start gazing at your inner compass.

Living like Air is a constant process of adjustment.

If your life is more consumed in work you need recreation. If you find that you are inactive, spend a little time being more active. Stretch the edges, explore the probabilities, participate in all the other activities. During weekends, pause for ten minutes from your routine, reflecting on what you need the most set some priorities, what you have done and what needs to be improved. Allot time to those perspectives that are important constantly adjustable important needs, making an appropriate tracking of improved skills of recognition of your choices in proper order so in the end it becomes self gratification and adds meaningful reason's to be in this blissful life.

You must take your place in
the Circle of Life as you were put on the earth for a reason.

Your role here is important to play, in constant adjustment and keep flowing like air in the world.

Don't get lazy and give up on things.

There are people that need you in their lives - you may be their only world. You should accept lessons on the way, reclaiming the process of life, you must learn from all the mistakes you make.

Take your place in the natural flow of things.
Everything you see exists
together in a delicate balance - you
need to understand that balance.
Everyone has a different story.
Everyone lives with a different concept.
Everyone's visualisation may differ, but you at your
place need to be firm, determined in self-belief.

Balancing the wants
Balancing the needs
Balancing the ultimate self-process of being very
calm and patient.

Live authentic and a true life, balancing like Air.

II. Compassionate Fire

Who said I can't?

- Silk Route
- The real test
- Every event offers you a lesson
- Pantheism, the truth
- Simplify your life
- Change
- Pearls of wisdom fire

9. Who said I can't?

Stand in Faith even when you are having the hardest time in your Life.
Don't Give up. You will find Sunshine flowing back through all dark lines.
Enhance your day one more time.
The responsibility to Make a Change lies with you.
All can be Reconstructed, Revived Again.
It's you who can, with a strong
Self-belief, Responsibility and self-esteem.
All this go hand in hand.

The more you have one, the more is the growth of the other.
Move Ahead - See the transformation in yourself.
Stay in positive momentum
Asking yourself,
Who said I Can't...
See the immensely powered positivity and immediate recognition of your strength within you.
You rise above the struggles,you acquire all the strength needed.

As every stumbling block can be sculpted into a
Timeless, Classical Statue
Only if the sculpture amalgamates Courage &
Determination.

10. Silk Route

The 3 P's Positive ~ perceptions ~persistent- Adoption of Positive Elements.

When we are dissolved in happiness, we live more, we are contented. We also take more positive decisions. We are able to face everything positively.
Because you are filled with positivity, you make positive vibes around you. You also gain more strength from within.
You're embedded in an enormous aura of positivity. So you ask all the related questions as to Where, How When? Things become more visible. Clarity is radiated in all impossible circumstances.
When you start directing your life in positivity, you take every challenge as a task.
You seek more opportunities in every task. The ability to face any test in life is incorporated here, now.
Now you see every corner that was once submerged in darkness -they are now glittering with new possibilities of solutions.

It is as if thousands of doors are being opened in reception to your affirmative approach. There is only one key ingredient - that is, of allowing positivity to bathe you in the effervescence of the positive recognition of yourself. You start investing in your moments. Being in positivity helps you revive the imperfect strings of your emotions into suitable and synchronized thoughts. Now you conquer all unsettled issues and try to pace them at ease. Because you're now at peace from within, and have regained trust in life through your positive feelings, experience the radiance of life.

Being in positivity and in peace, you are, as a catalyst, able to adjust to the ups and downs of life in a much easier and subtle way.

You become acquainted with your paths and you start embracing problems with enthusiasm. Miraculously, you see problems being transformed into tasks which you willingly take up as a challenge and a test to yourself.

Seeding positivity makes you grow and shine with optimism.

~ *Perceptions matter*

Everyday, we face enormous experiences. Just add on a very subtle reminder here that everything, whether good or bad, pain or pleasure, mistakes or achievements, name-fame-shame, approvals and disapprovals, happiness or sorrows,
all - each and everything shall

but pass away like one more passing show.
Like a day blends in night, it's the eternal truth that every beginning has an ending and that's the way it's supposed to be.
Don't live in captivating your past
worrying about those things which are gone. I see people around fretting over lost relationships or immersed in financial problems. Unknowingly, they are blocking potential which could otherwise become more constructive elements.
On an average, we get more than seventy thousand thoughts in a day out of which 95% are the thoughts which are associated with past issues. Now if we keenly introspect the mental dynamics we may be able to rectify all that is needed to be changed.
We need to reconstruct this. We need to reframe all our energy not in the past,but in the present, doing something concrete.
We have to replenish our perceptions into more defined strategies.
Every experience starts and finishes at a time.
Every thought arises, is explored,and subsides eventually. Emotions are raised, explored, settled; then perhaps they vanish. Everything gets replaced over a period of time. The process is designed in the beginning and endings.
We feel happy when all is perfect, but a tiny little change creates a complexity in our thoughts at once.
We are dissatisfied often - either if pleasure does not last

or if pain does not vanish.
We demand immediate solutions.
But subsequently everything that begins will eventually end at sometime.
Erase the habit of being worried unnecessarily.
Change your perceptions. Whatever has come, has to go.
A glass is made but shall eventually get shattered into infinitely small pieces.
Everything comes with a shelf life.
So instead of fretting over the past, start living in the present. Just remind yourself more often, that even this shall pass away and that nothing shall last forever.

~Believe in persistence

All the circumstantial challenges in life are but a process.
Start believing in the very meaningful probabilities - that all is a process. We have to live in the core of our own convictions, and have to adapt them. Challenge these in the form of growth. Perform to your very best, so as to overcome the hurdles on the way easily and
also, by only believing that everything has to be perceived in continuity.
Every element embedded has a great depth of meaning in this universe.
Everything is associated with factors that have a reason.

By believing the process of life, by having faith, by practising more of patience, raise the level of life, to harmony, to peace in wonderment.
Effective transformations are uninterrupted processes of life.
We will remain unhappy if we deliberately interfere in the natural flow of experience.
We have to believe that we have to face all the obstacles on the path of our lives. We need to rebuild the enormous positive potential needed to face these challenges. When we start inculcating the only possible positive perceptions in persistence we draw the needed change in order.
It's said when life gets difficult, you got to change your order and that is nothing but being even stronger to face it all. This impacts all that is associated.

Being positive, we emboss possible affirmations and do engage in only positive perceptions in persistence. So now, the question of being unhappy does not arises.

Everything is just matter of positive perceptions that too in persistence.

11. The Real Test

It's always the struggles and hardships that bring out the best qualities in you.
The real test starts in retrospect, when we rediscover ourselves thanks to our difficulties.
How we are able to learn from our trials and errors matters.

As it is said, failures are like fights in boxing rings - you are not defeated until you refuse to fight back...
We have to learn from failures - the real test starts here when our patience is tested.

Learn from your struggles.... When we go through hard times, we sometimes feel like giving up.
The moment that pushes you to give up should no longer be sheltered.
Just discard the thought as soon as it's born - instead try to focus on how far you have travelled.
Believe in the process of life.
Get acquainted with your paths - embrace your problems with more enthusiasm.

As problems arise, deal with them carefully instead of becoming impatient.
The real test is what we learn from our previous mistakes.
How much have we reconstructed our flaws, how much effort we did we put in to rectify them.

Seek the new opportunities that are on your way.
Reviving the broken strings is not so hard - you just need a little more courage, a little more enthusiasm seeded in determination.
Just seek the correct moment and convert it into opportunity.
Never give up.

Rise above the storms.
There is always a reason for all our problems, our failures.
There is a reason why we meet some people on our way.
There is a reason to everything.
We have to rise above the storms and understand some undefined questions - start exploring them in a more efficient way.
What went wrong?
Why did it occur?
Was it necessary?
Problems either make us grow or make us learn some more of life's tough lessons.
People come into our lives to make us see what we were unable to see earlier.

There can be many numbers of reasons, but every time, there's a lesson hidden in the last.
We have to learn from all. What you become depends on you - the moment you start taking initiatives to make a change by just overcoming your dark fears, everything changes forever.
Never stop trying and learning from your failures and from your mistakes

Appreciate that no matter how hard your life may be, just appreciate whatever you have now.
Your importance being in life will not decrease if someone out there does not recognise your abilities understand the concept and you become unstoppable start again in positive thoughts and recondition the process of your life.
Sometimes, it's good to react with no reaction at all. Be contented with what you have. Be commited to what you said and what you want to do in life. Start to live with tremendous positive passion and remain focussed on your goals.

Enjoy all the little happiness that is in store for you. It happens when you believe that anything is possible. ***The Responsibility to make a Change lies in you...***

12. *Every Event offers you a Lesson*

~~ Lessons learned...

Every event that appears more turbulent might reveal itself to be as park of unlimited opportunities to an opportunistic person.

That's the definition of perception.
Life offers subtle reminders in form of events that look like challenges or problems.

It's we who have to adapt a positive paradigm by erasing the habit of worry about things that may never happen.
We got to sublimate into pure possible affirmative scheme as a brief description of what you think about life instead of being sceptical at times of transitions.

We have to consistently redirect our minds to live in the present. You have to inculcate boundless energies clubbing together enthusiasm and courage to deal what so ever life portray for you more flamboyantly

Some of the lessons that life makes us learn is - who we are, and what we should be leaving behind after the transformation that we face out from all the hardships and the struggles. There is an infusions of self realisations rewinding your path in much more observations leading to purpose of living simultaneously surging virtues of enlightenment enriching your inner compass into more meaningful conception of life

Sometimes it is the opposite. There
will be struggle, there will be bad days which never seem to end. Days which go on and on, which keep us hurting till the end.
But being calm, being in patience delivers the exquisite wonders and offers you solutions in the simplest things with all the ecstasy you deserve.

Many of us are desperate as the mind gets flooded with millions of negatively charged thoughts during tough times. It times of hardship, most would give up - but the people who will not- will be the ones to face the brighter side of the day.
Instead of fretting over small things and complaining about past events, they utilise every present moment seeking different avenues to widen their own paths studded into millions of sparkling diamonds, making this lessons as miraculous sights leading them to self analysis, self approvals, self reminders, self leaders of their own destiny and master craftsmen of their own path creating their own destinies.

Remember always, that though the night is darkest before dawn,and no matter how cloudy and gloomy the sky, no matter how much it rains,there is always the rainbow afterwards, that brings in colour and happiness..

We must come to terms with the fact that no matter how hard we try to fit in this imperfect world, it will never acknowledge us for who we are.
We need to strive hard to fit in the frame with determination, self-belief, courage and enthusiasm.

Life lessons transform your life magnificently helping you to obtain more defined objectives, initiating self responsibility at every next level preparing you more willingly accepting the unpredictable challenges of life more efficiently.

Everyone wants to be happy at the end of the day...

Just enforce the steel of discipline; forge strong self-belief and start scaling success for a very peaceful and beautiful life.

13. Pantheism, the Truth

Everything is glorified with God's fingerprints

Our Life, our mind, our soul, our body... are like a beautiful garden. It symbolises harmonious glorification with joy, peace and happiness.
Many of us don't take enough responsibility for this magnificent event called Life.
We also make it toxic with self-created anxieties and worries.
Nurturing it everyday, in fears, in darkness,we injure our own souls. We unknowingly do injustice to the natural flow of life and thus
the process of life deteriorates into unending pains and agonies.
The only contentment that we find is when we seek peace within ourselves, when we seek calmness even when everything around us is in turbulence - but we at the centre are at peace.

When we are transformed while being at peace, our priorities and our inner selves are all in contentment.

We trade our life collecting achievements. But all these are only external rewards that we get by investing our precious life.
We continue searching for our goals, for getting promotions, earning money, getting praise, for recognition, but perhaps, these are all temporary.

The only contentment that we find is the peace of the inner self.

Here,we learn to stay at the centre at peace, redeeming our inner growth, gaining courage and confidence by learning the art of patience.
Not necessarily in proper format but things do change drastically. We unnecessarily make our souls toxic by being stressed, by being in depression and sweating the small stuff.
We have to shed our shackles of reason and start believing that everything that happens is so that we learn a lesson. Everything is marked with God's fingerprints.
Every event has a lesson, every setback offers improvements.
We have the potential to unlock lasting happiness.
We can cultivate enlightenment by seeking inner fulfilment and inner peace along with contentment.
Once we accomplish this, life is beautiful.
We start loving this life.
We see beauty in the sunrise, we see beauty in the snow-capped mountain.
We see beauty in every smile.

We feel at peace from within.
More glorified, more filled in contentment. We start celebrating the event called Life.
Now we can see the differences between the positives and negativities. We realise that negativity actually does not exist and that we choose it during our failures our and hardships, nurture it to make it grow.
Perhaps the time could have been utilised with more positive enthusiasm. Once we see that everything has God's fingerprints on it, every time we can learn something and move forward instead of standing in the same place and becoming stagnant.

Struggling in negativities, we are actually webbing our inner selves and restraining the growth of life and happiness.
We can eventually safe guard our garden by restricting these negative thoughts and fears to enter our minds and we need to prevent the negativity from growing.
Making our soul, our mind, our life more peaceful more contented, more flowing in oceans of love and happiness. Thus we start growing from in, seeking truth of life and start seeking happiness and peace by redeeming more of being in patience and ***start living a more meaningful life.***

14. Simplify Your Life

You have the Simplify Life- rebuild into new dimensions from within, draining all the negatives. Complexity can be cut back. We can make choices for a simpler life. Needs versus wants can be focussed on limitations. Simplify your life – yes, the less you desire, the more contented you are from within. No one is holding a gun to your head saying that you must complicate life. Everyone can revive and control life and convert it into more time. Start controlling your thoughts, expanding the edge of possibilities and refuelling the power to influence, hence restructuring our actions to excel in performances.

Every day, I hear so many people experiencing dis satisfaction in life. It's all about how you cannot fit into the frame and eventually feel disheartened;for you are unable to face what's on the path of Life.

And, of course, what they think, what they assume, what they perceive... comes about as the result. And the hardships become an unending saga.

But there are two words that have a tremendous effect on your life and that can redirect, redeem the insurmountable circumstances, making them favourable - once you start using them...

..I Will

...When you learn a new idea, your inner belief transitions into self-confidence, encouraging you to say, "I will."...When you learn a new idea to raise your inner belief starts in transitions into self confidence, and encouraging you to say "I Will make this my goal with a little more focus and devotion more in continuity and immense of practice."

Regain positivity with peace, clearing out all the dark fears of uncertainties. When someone offers you an opportunity to work, when you look more towards your performance say, "I will get this done better, more smoothly and efficiently."

...When you face hardships or confront a problem say, "I will turn this into a challenge and see this as a growth."

Relatively what you perceive will be implemented as the performing abilities are the things you focus on.

We don't really see the things the way they are. We see things through our inner perceptions.

Look for good. Search for the truth seed. Be positive and see the transition in whatever you do.

That's the way the brain works.
Look for success as a ladder, step by step, and you'll get it. It's not a mere mystical influenced concept.

It's what you teach your brain to conceptually build -a strong, internal stimuli that keeps accelerations more in positive affirmations with words I Will...

It's just to Simplify life of Complexity reclaimed in more bright opportunities by the add on of peace, patience, self-belief. Expecting less and delivering more of yourself into more dimensions transforms all failures into lessons of growth.

Don't forget that your strength lies in the choices that you make.

15. Change

A change is the most difficult phase of Life.

Never underestimate power of persistence.
It is persistence that creates the incredible change that you're seeking. Change gives you a chance to get out of your comfort zone.
It adds growth.
Nurtures experience, exploring great new paths to walk.
The hardest of all is to let go.
The moment we decide to move ahead leaving behind things we can't change, it requires immense courage.
We keep struggling to hold on.
That serves no meaning.
We struggle to let go. This time is critical we need to make choice in affirmations that serves Life of prosperity Life of Happiness Life of Growth Life is a great book that teaches us all aspects of the most important things in our lives. It can sometimes lie to us and no one will even notice. It can play all sorts of games with us, without us even knowing it, because

there is no one controlling it. But whatever happens in life happens for some reason and perhaps good.

Whatever decisions life takes for us is already planned by it long before we understand it. We must learn to accept it rather than behaving as a refrained recipient we must
come to terms with the fact that no matter how hard we try to fit in this imperfect world, no matter how hard it is to keep the pace flowing, still we have to keep moving. It will never acknowledge us for who we are. But everyone wants to be happy at the end of the day.
We strive hard to make our life peaceful and tranquil and continuously make efforts to ensure that everything goes well.
And we start making best of our inputs throughout the stormy nights, throughout the lonely days, throughout all the cold memories seeking calmness peace perfection. We embrace life as it comes, making us stronger to live for another day.
Being positive makes all things work in smooth flow.

Fly like an Eagle - concentrate on achieving peace.

Focus on getting peace of mind.

...this not only reduces the risk of failures but allows you to choose your battles more wisely. Some people in our lives are just energy drainers and are not worth to be within the frame your life. Your life is most precious, most valuable - so unless there's something much more important at stake, don't waste efforts trying to change situations or convince a person who is negatively entrenched. As the saying goes, you can't fly like an eagle if you're walking like a turkey. So make sure that if you are surrounded by these energy drainers - make a change it is better to be proactive than to be reactive.

For a greater change in life minimize misunderstandings and misinterpretations, engage more putting efforts on solving problem do not stretch the conversations if you feel offended by someone's words or actions or deeds try to gaze their situation before the final verdicts avoid all unnecessary issues keep away from negatives get desired results widening your perspectives often plays an important role during a much needed change.

Just try to seek the truth make sure all statements do not execute irresponsible behaviour they must be dealing with lots of other life issues. Make a simple at your approach and try to hear the person more, make the required change if you can or just let it be as it is for some time, that is also one of the most simple catch to avoid unavoidable circumstances towards the change needed.

Pick your battles wisely, save your time and avoid problems. Not all the situations are permanent.

16. *Pearls of Wisdom – Element, Fire*

Some storms in life leave behind deteriorated and damaged paths which are full of uncertainties but dare to find where they lead Surrendering to challenges doesn't work, participation is a must. Everyone knows that the paths to success are scattered with struggles, delays that are sometimes unexplained - but you need to board the flight with confidence and courage and be compassionate to fellow travellers.
The moment which prompts you to
give up should no longer be sheltered.
Discarding the negatives, look back to see how far you have travelled.

Conditioned in unawareness, many people just don't realise the power of their minds. They spend most of their lives reliving past events. Enthusiasm and courage are the keys to glow as fire while you are still cruising.

Redirect all your energies into goal setting and compiling defined objectives to make your life magnificently more magical.
Cultivate inner discipline and remember every setback offers equivalent opportunities to learn and grow. The best way to drive your life is like driving an automobile - keeping the balance of mind, using your skills in patience. The triangulation of positive perception in persistence leads new graph of life. Everything works seamlessly beautiful

If you're shattered, broken by circumstances, by pain, just let God take care of you. He will himself heal you. Remember even broken pieces, if studied minutely, occupy some shape, some place becoming something very different and very new, different from its original form. So you must embrace all such devastating situations since they came to you, to help you rediscover yourself.

You just need to wait patiently.
Let God craft a new you.
So let your fire of being compassionate and being in patience glow effortless through out the life. Don't allow rejection or failures overtake you - instead let them motivate you. Hearing a 'No' isn't end of the world. Take it as a piece of information which tells you that you don't belong here. Start working for better options, rediscover yourself and focus on new horizons.

Just be filled with enthusiasm like Sun which shows up every morning spreading enormous energy to each and every corner bearing all still glowing all the sides to the fullest extent with a beautiful message to glow in faith live in hope that life is available only in this moment.
Being in compassion is like trying to light a fire while outside in a storm, you need to protect the match-flame from being blown out and when it has grown enough to burn a candle in dark, you still need to protect it until the fire is visible growing itself. In this the flame is compassionate it tends to burn with all its strength. The light is so easily lost and blown out if there is again a strong wind.

Being sincere being in patience play tremendous role during the hard times while you still be firm believing that everything will be fine. Sincere towards your faith Patience towards your results

Be compassionate like the fire.

III. Courageous Water

What if I adapt more courage?

- ✦ I have learned to smile
- ✦ Oasis of life
- ✦ Palette of serenity
- ✦ Life is to live, in courage
- ✦ In God's grace
- ✦ Being responsible at the end of the day
- ✦ Pearls of wisdom ~ Water

17. What if I Adapt more Courage?

The challenges that you have met are behind you. As the day departs, some of us do miss opportunities, some of us are down due to failed relationships or setbacks at the workplace. Most of us complain and whine about our problems. We can restore them instead, by using time, in our favour. Remember, life is always in progress.

Perhaps now you will find all the new opportunities ahead.

So what if you adapt some more courage and strengthen yourself to endure the most difficult situations?

90% of failures are not because people were defeated, it's because people quit.

When you redeem more of your self-belief, more of your courage, you flow significantly more like ripples of water. Every champion was once a contender who refused to give up. Every setback is a blessing that signifies that something better is in store for you.

Adapt more courage and defy the daily grind that weighs you down.
Focus on what you want, what you are passionate about... discarding all uncertainties and by infusing a little more courage into your life.

Keep flowing in Courage like ~Water...

18. I have learnt to Smile

I've learnt to just smile, instead of being in constant pain.
At times, people suggest that the best antidote to pain is to keep on trying be in hope always be in positive thoughts. As it is the definition of the hardships to commiserate and stand in all odds instead of surrendering.
Live physically active life. But I know I'm on to something. I can't afford to waste my beautiful life. I need to do my best to spread the smiles.
Besides all the time I'm here to keep walking somehow. Most mornings I feel that I haven't been able to make the best of my life. There is so much to be done yet.
Some days it gets easier, others it doesn't. That's the way it is. You just have to keep going, accomplish what you perceive in your thoughts and to make the best of it. I think one of the main benefits of writing

is that it makes you to think positively. You can't think negatively.
There's no easy way down the mountain.

Some among us make it look so easy.
I call it water-rippling – smart performers make excellence look effortless and seem to make things happen as gracefully as a ripples move along the water.

But like water, you need to keep flowing in all circumstances. What you don't get to see is all the hard-work taking place inside the busy minds.
The best way for spectacular results is to practise a little courage every day, breeding positive thoughts.
In my life, I have a learnt that an abundance of patience is the only key to success.
Apart from this continued sessions of practices that set up all the great canvas of life super shine making every day a great day. Yes, sometimes life sends you back into unexpected challenges that knock you off the path -that's just life. It's a temporary phase in transit happening.
Keep positive and practise overcoming fear. But with a series of only positive concepts and overcoming fears practices to keep you at your best, you'll stay in a positive state much more often
Fear are scary sometimes
Unpredictable but When it surfaces, we are reluctant to interconnect and are sure seeking tremendous

possibilities and wired to run away unknowingly avoiding it to consider it as a lesson of growth

In my mind, fear is beautiful. It multiplies and is an opportunity to examine my own potential - it's like a gift.

If you run away from your fear, you run from your brightest inner compass. In contrast to the fact every fear that is keeping you small is your own popped up thought results in least possibility of overcoming your ability your authenticity greatness to over caste the best way out of it.

To Seek away distance from your fear is to run from the brightest inner compass of yourselves

you were meant to be a great navigator moving in confidence Fears are nothing more than doorways into better versions of your own inner capabilities, your own transiting phase a search for brighter vision to things that scare you to move ahead in confidence.

Life portrays spectacular opportunities to discover more of all you all in blend of hardships fears uncertainties. Fear isn't bad. Sometimes, it reinvents you into an all-new person.

It's good. It helps you build courage and confidence, giving you self-respect. It makes you shine better and reach for success.

Leading to insurrections of Continuous courage building the prospective of confidence confirming your move that Leads to; Self believe, Self respect Self analysis that leads in Promoting Growth and Makes you better.

And you Shine in excel in glory of Success.

19. Oasis of Life

Socrates Once Said:
The unexamined life is not worthy living.

Life ***can't*** be seamlessly flowing always. There's a continuous flow of joys and sorrows, creating a sort of inner compass always in requisitions of more convenient parameters as though nudging you gently towards reinventing your destiny each time.
While sometimes the circumstantial challenges nurture us to behave more pragmatic making us more available. Once we introspect on our lives, we try to venture out of our cocooned ordinary inner self existences to explore contentment. Ultimately, life is a reflection of all the choices we have made on our way.
Desires coupled with integrated intellect may further sense all the eagerness of reaching towards success in more disciplinary methods.

More succinctly the phrase oasis of life can be defined as: The only people who are truly enlightened are the one who experience the bliss of daily tackling all their problems, as lessons for their inner growth. They resolve to live more in harmony with all aspects of an unpredictable life.

The simple strategy here is to over come all fears as they take root in your mind.

To overcome failures, to seek lessons in all your struggles and your hardships.

Most influential people have cemented their legacies by overcoming fears of failure.

They tried every time more seeded in passion and determination after every fall. Fears are just conditional responses to our impulses that drive us towards negativity. Fears often consume all our positive energies, our enthusiasm... and our desire to grow is halted. Actually, fears are created by you yourself. If we should choose to overcome our fears with strong willpower, we can overcome the dark fears while

comprehending that failures are a necessary part of life. They are essential for growth in our lives. We can always redeem the process of life by actually recognizing failures and hardships as common. We should willingly accept the paradigm of uncertainties and allow ourselves to be changed by our hardships and failures. This should not come as surprise - that every struggle actually shapes us into a new individual who is closer to accepting responsibility. We can genuinely find growth in our failures.

One of the finest quality redirected on the edge of

our failures is we get experiences which are most precious that can't be rendered by any faculties to be more precise. Life itself becomes our learning ground,to make us more responsive towards our proposed dreams and understanding our weaknesses. Nurturing the thought, I personally feel that we should let go of factors that are beyond our control. One of the profoundly influenced positive fuelled thought is, to seed some courage to let go of things that can't be changed. When we are in hardship, we are disturbed and insecure. But when we do discover the reverse process, we find that actually all the pains, struggles, hardships and sorrows are helping us to grow into a high level of patience, peace and perseverance.

Once we overcome our fear, we set our priorities for more enthused efforts. Fears are easily shattered,resulting in enormous confidence,courage and happiness.

We can be fully free from worries or we can attain the quality of being fearless always is unequivocal quest though.

Self-belief, Ambitions, Perceptions Determination, Will-power can all enforce the Change required for Success.

Self negligence, unbalanced thinking are also responsible for the tides of Uncertainties.

Thus the Oasis of life can ceaselessly and

continuously flow in reverence that Life starts when we come out of our comfort zones.

With time, things that were once impossible start to break down,
changing and making our paths remarkably more easy to walk on.

20. Palette of Serenity

3 S' of Serene Life

Seek stillness in serenity

We continue to live this life without tasting the nectar of truth. We are just slaves to our impulses, driving the vehicle of our body, soul and mind in different directions, unknowingly redeeming only unhappiness and keeping ourselves deprived ourselves of being in this serene life in true sense and ignoring the fact of purposeful living.
We are missing the key to our inner enlightenment by wasting our time and a tremendous amount of energy in just existing.

Seek

Do we seek any transformations for better and improvised living?
No, we hardly care.
We are like waves on a sea shore, struggling against a big rocky shore, waiting for the tides to take us in any direction.

If we try to seek and try to self-analyse the core cause of our delays and failures in life, we can find the important segment that was missing.
Self-analysis directs us to restrain the unwanted negativities seeded deeply in our minds. We have seeded this negativity for years and have allowed it to spread.

Stillness

Making us slaves to our impulses, making us reactive during uncertainties, leading only to failures and unhappiness...
Now that we know our flaws, we should willingly accept and try to rectify them as soon as possible.
We need to develop a deep sense of safe-guarding our negative thoughts. We can now develop the ability to discard an unwanted and a nagging thought, as soon as it pops up in our mind.

Instead of becoming slaves to our habits, we can now be master of our own thoughts - driving the vehicle of our mind, soul and body to move very much from inside, by being more calm, by seeding more patience, and by seeking the true meaning of being in this Life. The palette is given to you. Now you choose the colours to be filled in - serenity is your choice.

Acquire the necessary skills, like that of being more in calmness rather than reacting to your surroundings.

Also, continuous fostering of positive thoughts makes an incredible change.
Seeking peace, seeking inner growth, seeking contentment - all flights are into designated paths now.
Cultivate willpower in abundance by continuing to work against negative impacts and erasing unwanted weak thoughts. We can focus on a more positive approach, focus on positive probabilities, resulting in prosperity and delighted atmosphere around you.

Serenity

Make better choices of serenity by incorporating the colours of gratitude, calmness, being a good listener, patience, kindness, and also eradicating the habit of being in worries always.
Yes, now you have the palette, you have the colours, make an incremental improvement, producing lasting results of living this life in magnificence in radiance more in glory.
Encouraged attitudes towards making more of your willpower strong everyday is like placing brick over a brick while making a room for living in peace. Once your willpower is enhanced, it escalates all your energy to act courageously.
Your confidence is rooted now.
You make your life more serene, more meaningful -the process of life becomes more adaptable.

Always remember that there is tremendous power in Stillness, in being calm, in being in patient, in silence, and that you accumulate all the serenity required to be in this life. Now this makes you able to cleanse your thoughts and you are now accredited to be the master of your own DESTINY...

Stillness is like a catalyst and connects you to the sources of wisdom in every little thing around you. Silence filled with stillness brings a radiant opportunity to live in more joyfulness enchantment towards more of happiness that now shines on your soul and your body too.
We start loving this life, we start seeking beauty in every little thing, we start being in gratitude, enhancing the quality of our life.

And we believe in the process of life, thus living a more meaningful life.

21. Life is to live in Courage

Life shrinks or expands depending on the proportions of our courage.

If you find yourself surrounded in darkness, just retrieve a little strength and bring in a thought that this situation is just like that of a caterpillar waiting in the dark for its colourful wings to grow.
Waiting builds positivity, helping you gain inner strength, encouraging you the most excellent perceptions of life and that is being in patience.
Confidence propelled in layers of ambitions helps in remarkable transitions.
It's just the act of courage and confidence now that makes the roots of Prosperity go deeper and make you stand in encouraged affirmations also making you stand , amidst of storms in dedications.
Confidence makes you believe in the process now.
Rejections can be resolved, for setbacks are placed often on the path of life. Some things don't work out the way we want them to. So how do you respond at this time - do you get depressed?

Do you start blaming yourself?
At this juncture, don't delude yourself into thinking that failures are your fault. Remember, you learn from mistakes. Unsettled in thoughts often People take defeat as guilt, shaping it as their final destiny. Rejections spell failure only if you don't believe in yourself. Don't waste time searching for perfection in yourself; live in courage for that's more important. Accept that we are like everyone else – a mixed blend of capabilities and limitations.

In your darkest hour, never worry that there's no hope for the future. You are the author of your own destiny, you get to decide the next chapter.
The best strategies to be adapted have been given to you as 'advice' below:

Segmentation to the best adapted strategies at the difficult times revalued into small pockets of energy boost lined up as advisements below. Make a best suited adaption keep living in courage.
Try to be cheerful. Do what makes you happy. When we are happy from inside we live life and make our surroundings a better place.
Do not ignore your health - keep track of your eating habits. Drink lots of water. Practice meditation. Grab time from your busy schedule for being in silence.
It re-energises the body, mind and soul, creating a balance.

Music adds healing to life processes.
It rekindles old memories and provides a connection to untold
happiness. Music soothes our soul and our body and not only helps to heal
the wounded heart, but also helps to express the deepest emotions. Music energizes our
inner being - it elevates and uplifts our consciousness.
Music makes our lives more meaningful and complete.
It stimulates all our nerve cells.

"One good thing about music, when it hits you, you feel no pain." – Bob Marley.

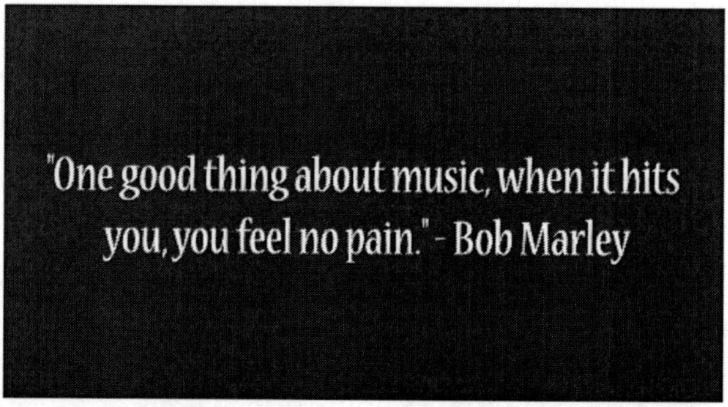

Get yourself more organized. Read good books stay away from all those things that make you unhappy or those that serve no reason to be in your life.

Life means to move on constantly, growing each day with wisdom, acquiring all good thoughts and spreading love, making this world a better place

22. *In Gods TIME*

Living in God's timing is the only truth that connects us to Him.
I observed this through many odds in life when circumstances were inevitable hardships not diluting instead I used to think that life is getting worse.
The immediate dilemma was "I don't know what to do". After great deliberation, I finally arrived to the quietness of my inner self which reflected and came to the conclusion that being in God's grace can settle all the things that are churning like a whirlpool.

Looking back at my childhood days, I remember those afternoons during the summer vacations which I used to spend in playing with broken colourful glass bangles. Those were blissful, serene days when quality time was spent playing on mango and guava trees.
I would collecting broken pieces of bangles and would try to arrange them by pasting each broken piece on a white cardboard sheet, giving it new floral patterns.

Looking back, I really can understand God's true Grace that despite matters that made me shatter, I did feel broken, but God's grace and His faith kept me going.
I knew he would arrange all the broken pieces by giving them a new form, much better than the original.

Sometimes things keep
Delaying. This makes us
Vulnerable. We feel unprotected.
It's God's interventions
that protect us from
dangers that we don't see.

Just understand and trust God.
But there's a difference.
To trust, to understand. .

When we trust God, we willingly accept all that is played out in our lives.
When we understand, we clearly perceive his will and his wisdom; we then can take pleasure and pain as equally important.
We connect with him closely.

... People often blame others for their failures or if some things are not working in their lives. They never look at their own shadows which drag them into light of awareness light of consciousness. When they accept the truth when they change the perception things starts to change. They grow in and out step towards better living with clear concise adding meaning to their lives.

God is the serenity weaver of our life and when he is standing with you it does not matter who is against you.

23. *Being Responsible at the End of the Day*

Hard times, difficult phases, are meant to rearrange our lives with an incredible gift of lessons from life. Nature is an amazing teacher. Life is run by Nature's Rules. You may have observed the collection of cacti in the desert that bloom into a magnificent array of flowers.
Pearls of lives which are indeed like uncertainties and also the Rough conditions often bring precious gifts. Life can be hard. We all have our good seasons as well as difficult ones. But hard times bring many blessings as well as equally important lessons that are essential for the life in order to strengthen the perspectives self-awareness and courage.

Be determined and let your burning passion help you achieve your goals.
Some of the qualities of the very best leaders that have walked before us are to be screened every time you're in difficulties

No one was a born leader or a born artist, or writer. They made their paths practicing their passions, giving their best.
We grow the most as human beings during our roughest times. So why do we judge them as being bad?
When they bring transformations, these challenging pieces of our lives just might be when we are most alive. And they always bring tiny miracles. If you are awake to them.

Your decisions, your likes, your dislikes, your circumstances - all reflect as your personality.
You will become your surroundings. So choose them wisely.
Re-channelling things that you are associates with and the choices that you make can eventually shape your thinking and your actions.
Sometimes, it's hard to digest when our dreams shatter. The immediate question is "Why?"

We start to analyse all the good outcomes that are now unavailable, that are now overshadowed by volumes of negative thoughts emptying all the self believe that was clubbed in the process.
We often intercept with Why did God postponed this question is inevitable.

The truth is that God is still working to place you on a better path.

We need to closely connect with him to believe in his wisdom.
Sure, we have missed opportunities but most of us just complained.
But at the end of the day, we need to be responsible.

We are a work in progress. We are given another great day to fulfil all that we want to.
Just be grateful, be responsible and work towards your goals with all determination.

24. *Pearls of Wisdom ~ Water*

Vista of a Beautiful Life~

We are all made up of life force in the form of energy, which connects us to the realm of calmness rather than reacting to your surroundings. This energy fuels everything into our priorities and surmount into great manifestations. And to speak all this energies subsequently redeem a culture of being in transparency.

Enlightened from within, we follow the concepts to treat everyone around us in dignity and decent reforms. More specifically mind body, soul are coined into peaceful submissive guidelines virtually in respect to decisions made from the odysseys of life which had been unsealed uncertain at times.

Let the coffer of life be conceived and compiled by the major and most filled with the precious key ingredients like hope, faith, peace, patience, kindness and gratitude.

If you feel stressed at times and feel dejected, you are far away from the centre of contentment.
This is the core, the pure, the mystical vortex of being in peace.

If you believe in a little positivity, you inculcate and infuse a little hope and you are close enough to that vortex of peace, the core element of contentment.

If you seed faith, you can cultivate all the keys that emblem the path of being in harmony with yourself, and endorsing self catering redemption of changes in your life.

Being in peace does not mean being at a place where there is no noise. It means that we are in peace even if we are surrounded by hardships and entangled in failures. But we still have the ability to stand up, restoring all the broken blocks, trying to re-energise our inner self.

This truth brings about the enthusiasm for a new beginning.
Thus, hope, peace and faith are essential segments of this amazing life.

Being kind offers the core meaning to this life.
The more kind you are, the more energy resonates, radiating a positive aura. The very purpose of life is solved here.

Being in gratitude draws you closer to faith - the next step - of becoming closer to God.

Forgiveness is the best form of love. We can relatively rise the dynamics of the unattainable probabilities into positive possibilities.

Thus the process of life is recreated into a key catalyst for measuring the quality of life

Being in peace, being in patience but moving... being in transparency - flowing like water. Colourless,Pure,Serene...Flowing,Quenching and still not losing its Identity.

IV. Grateful Earth

Am I being in Patience?

- ✦ Peace-maker.
- ✦ Re-orienting ourselves.
- ✦ Rediscover.
- ✦ This too shall pass.
- ✦ Being at peace.
- ✦ Time to move on.
- ✦ Pearls of wisdom ~ Earth

25. Am I being in Patience?

Life has many unexplained ways of testing us. We may find it difficult at times to even move one step forward.
We are occupied by negative thoughts flooding us, generating more failures.

Just relax and take a deep breath.

Nothing lasts forever.

During such devastating situations, be calm. Try not to take important decisions as they are effectively submerged in other factors.
Just remain calm at your core, even if all is at turbulence in the outside world.
Keep the faith and trust and be patient.
You will find a way out when you are calm and patient.

Keep moving, Grateful like ~ Earth.

26. The Peace Maker

Let Go... Move On - Re-Orient ~

We tend to spend a lot of time ruminating about what's wrong with life. We often complain about the injuries that left scars deeply rooted in our minds.

We complain to others about our struggles, our pains.
Sometimes, we are hurt deeply.
We tend to hold on to little resentments that must have taken root during arguments or misunderstandings.

The way we nurture painful events very close to our hearts should be keenly introspected.

When we encounter such a painful phase, we often try to put ourselves into a remote zone. We stubbornly wait for someone else to reach out to us first.
This is not the only way that perhaps could be utilized to rekindle a broken heart or a broken relationship.

We tend to generate more hate, more anger by delaying the parameters which should have been pacified immediately should have been done immediately after a heated argument.
We start to build our positions into supreme transactions
If we keenly observe, we can see that it is very important to be happy than to be right, at times.
The only way to be happy is
~ Let go...

If you are really seeking happiness and peace, you should first understand others more.
Being right is never important but being happy is...
Let others be right most of the time...

In any arguments or misunderstandings, be the first to reach out and seek an apology.
Everything becomes alright over a period of time.
We experience the immediate effect of being at peace.

Letting go brings inner satisfaction. It's like self-liberation and acts in re-orientation of our beliefs by removing any grudge from deep inside the mind.

This brings a positive outcome since you know that you have done your part to create a tranquil, balanced atmosphere around you and being in harmony with yourself you are now endorsing self peace.

Restore your energies by redirecting them in a positive relationship building mechanism.

All relationships are needed to be perceived in reverence.
A trust embedded string of strong bond is thus regenerated once more

So instead of nurturing resentments, that stemmed out in due course of life start diluting the process by letting Go.....
Always try to be resilient after any unsettled circumstances. Trees that grow straight upn ever provide any shelter. The more you reach out, spread out in your gratitude, the more you affirm love and peace...
Don't wait for that perfect day that will never come. Restoration of peace and love is possible at any time...

In a nutshell, the golden words are...
Rejuvenating the process
Regaining the trust
and
Restoring again, serenity and hope in relationships.

And now
Live life before life leaves you.

The only mantra for a peaceful living...

Let Go, Move On...

27. Re-orienting Ourselves

Reminiscences - Re-orienting life.

When we are happy, we feel the essence of life beyond words. Thoughts flow clear and we feel full of energy.
When we gear up to be happy, we feel the serenity of life from within and we laugh, we smile,
we feel the grace of life,we see beauty everywhere.

Our serotonin levels, the neurotransmitters that are involved in nerve impulses, are elevated.
These neurotransmitters are directly related to our moods.
Lower levels cause depression, irregular sleeping patterns and also loss of appetite. But once we choose to safeguard our priorities, we can choose to be happier.
Laughter permeates every single cell of your body.

Practically speaking, we can, inculcate step–by-step, redemption of changes more significantly erase the habits of worrying all the times and enjoy optimism in true sense. Focus on good deeds, seeding positivity around you. Be cheerful always, directly challenging all the negative aspects, and make a tremendous change.

The thought of CHANGE must be seeded only by you. Trials and errors make you grow from your inner self. Re-orienting ourselves is not very hard. We can change many lives around us.
How many times do we accept our flaws and try to rectify them?

A little courage is needed to accept the mistakes that we do.
A little of awareness in the form of self-study and self-analysis is required.
When we face some problems or blocks on our path, it's just because we are restrained to move further at the wrong place at the wrong time. Engage yourself to redirect yourself onto a better path.

Learn to drive from with in just like automobile - you will see many things clearly.
Be at peace even when things go wrong, don't get messed up in the factors which cause delays or which bring failures.
It's just matter of time when everything is bound to happen precisely in accuracy in time set right.

Sometimes courage echoes in a very small voice at end of your failures saying

'Try once more in a different way'..
You can have whatever you are seeking with a little of courage to make some changes, determined to get the be stand with only your own self Belief.

No one can stop you.
As long as we have hope, tomorrow waits for us.
Being at peace is the inner energy that get transformed into positive perceptions which further may fuel as self manifestations an inheritance that unfolds all the limitless ways.

So instead of fretting over the past, start living in the present. For life is Awesome.

28. Rediscover Yourself

Self-esteem is enveloped in responsibility

Search for the Missing Elements

Engaged in our daily schedules.
We often find ourselves fixed at the same place.
We start cultivating more worries, in fact sometimes we don't hesitate screening our problems, our struggles into highest monumental descriptions and find ourselves unable in taking concrete decisions.
We are focused on negativity; in building lethargy.
So tiredness is just what you seeded in your mind.
This bad habits were indeed cultured by you when you had some difficult or tedious task. You always tried to prefer shortcuts instead of taking straight route of working hard no matter how much it gets delayed.

Now here are the applications to the truth.
All that you seek outside is in fact within you, it's your own inner self that makes you aware of what can go possibly right and what would be wrong. It is

all your choice to take a chance for the changes that you are seeking. You have to Rediscover yourself one more time while facing what so ever is on the route, is there ~
It's absolutely fascinating here when we Re discover our potentials curbing in disciplines camouflage into distinctive chromatographic insertions of words of hope, words of faith and words of self determination.

The key ingredient is your Will Power.

Re-bound - The Base; Encrust with Steel of Focused Enthusiasm

Our mind waits for our instructions
we need to actively cultivate disciplinary methods.
Each time you feel you have failed, you feel like giving up just curb the impulse and proactively neglect and erase the elements wrapped in negative thoughts into more positive thoughts. The more you control yourself, the more you can define the power of being the master of your inconvenient thoughts.
Set your goals and feel privileged to be in this life.
In such small victories, you will find a convergence of positive conceptions.

Now you synchronize all the will power you have, now double your willpower, you will work towards your self-esteem. Remember responsibility and self-esteem walk together in the same direction.

Set your resolutions.... Overcome your fears

This resolutions can be as simple as getting up early or even being quiet for five to ten minutes in midst

of your work thinking of nothing, deep breathing, for five to ten minutes; or even switching off the TV, or taking the staircase instead of the elevators.
When your simple goals are set, and you work more toward getting positive outcomes you see small victories shining giving you your much expected and enhancing results you start building more trust with yourself.
A thought process redirects your mind to all that have started working in your favour.

When you start managing your habits more efficiently, you will find it very easy. Just a more substantial and active approach is needed to redirect, to reform to rediscover your inner self.
Responsibility and your Self-Esteem needs to be mastered carefully as both are essential and perhaps self responsibility and self esteem walk on the same path in same directions.

Your persona is more refined, more radiant and can easily erase negative thoughts.
You now know how to keep worry at bay and you decide to walk independently on the route which you resisted before.
Align willpower with discipline and courage to re-generate your self-esteem forever.

The responsibility of your self-esteem is empowered by you Make it shine in radiance forever.

29. This Too Shall Pass ~ It Will

We can muster hope in the midst of despair

We live increasingly stressed life styles. Our own moods can be extremely deceptive during negative times, reflecting the bad shadows lowering our self-esteem.

Optimism helps combat gloomy times,offering courage and energy to shed the shackles of fear in adversity.
Remember, life teaches us all.
When we are in a good mood, life looks great.
Conversely, when our mood is bad, we start believing that life is worse and harder than it really is.

When you are in a good mood, we tend to be happy we have great perspectives our wisdom enlarges to see everything beyond perfection and we try to search in more positive avenues trending to reach destinations soon and in affirmations.
When we are in a good mood our thoughts get elevated to see good we feel good and we bring a lot

of positive energy. We see problems as challenges and they seem much easier to solve.

One of the best accomplishments during a good mood is the improvement in our communication. This is the best part which scales all the strategies a new meaning. If you're criticised, you will take it in your stride.

On the other hand, when you're depressed and in a bad mood or are feeling low, life looks unbearable and indeed more difficult.
You have very little perspective. You start taking things too personally and at times, often misunderstand those around you.

We have to distract ourselves from depressing thoughts.
Reject unnecessary, negative assumptions.
Try to write down your fears and your negative thoughts on paper, to try to sort out possible causes.

Try to find out what really matters. Determine the root of your discouraging thoughts. Just eliminate them as they pop up.
Share your concerns with the people you love. Talk out your problems.
Let them help you.
The truth remains that life is never bad - it's just some unavoidable circumstances. Remind yourself, that you are feeling stressed, a bit negative or frustrated because it's just a small bad mood. 'I

feel negative when I'm low.' This will pass - it is another transition of moods, an unavoidable human condition that will pass with time.

Remember, a low mood is not the correct time to analyse your life.
Just be grateful in your good times.
And be graceful in your bad times.
The next time you feel low for whatever reason, just tell yourself it's just an emotional wave passing in frequent heights of ups and downs and shall soon pass away
leaving behind calmness and peace forever.
When it's dark, you can see the stars.

Believe in yourself.

Have the courage to stand no matter what.

Remember that courage is the only key to stand against whatever is weighing you down.

30. Being at Peace

Life has many unexplained ways of testing you.
At times, we find it difficult to move even one step forward as we are unable to think out the problems that we may be facing since
we are occupied by negative thoughts flooding us and generating more failures.
Just relax, take a deep breath.
Nothing lasts forever.
During such situations, be calm and try not to take important decisions.
Just remain calm inside even if all outside is turbulent.
Keep the faith and trust and be patient.
You will find a way out when you are calm and at peace.

Every struggle makes you shine and moves you closer to your success.
Everything happens for a reason.
Every event has a lesson hidden.
When facing failures and hardships, don't give up.

Continuous efforts with courage and self-belief are the key to unlock your hidden *potential.*
Sometimes, courage speaks in a small voice at the end of your failures saying,

"Raging storms are always there but eventually, by being patient and calm, we can be in peace.
Try not to react to things as and when they happen."
All the actions and circumstances
have no power over you unless you react. It is useless if you keep taking unnecessary tension and drain your energy. Just let it be. Think about
the lesson that the situation has offered and learn from the hard times.
Be grateful even if all isn't well.
Be in Peace. Forget about the unavoidable circumstances.
Be yourself. Create yourself. Spend time on being at peace. Keep positive thoughts, engage in work.
We should probably seek the simplest form of strategic approach where peace dwells and offers you calm.
Our mind is not at peace only because it does not let go and urges you to hold on to perceptions.
This results in suffering, stress and discomforts, adding disappointment.
Hence, we need to see how effectively we can be in peace in spite of our many troubles.
Thus we seek high levels of happiness.

Our mind lacks being in peace because only disturbed thoughts can emerge from negatively charged issues or people. So focus on calming our nerves for being patient delivers peace.

'Try Once again in a different way.'

So believe in the process.
You can have whatever you are seeking if you are ready to struggle. So structure your confidence and believe in determination.

What you seek lies on the other side of the Dark Fears. Never give up. Keep trying - being at peace gives magnificent results.

31. Time to Move On

Lasting happiness is a powerful paradigm of life when I turn the pages of my past.
When we effectively set definite aims for ourselves, pursuing courage and reacting less to things as they happen, we can really make doors open to enlightenment.
Whenever we are coping with stressful situations like a disappointment of some kind, most of us choose to adversely react in a way that does not serve us. Then we overreact till we blow things out of proportion. We tend to hold on to the negative impact too closely immobilising the positive attributes.

We are bothered about things which may happen, we get irritated or annoyed easily, and lose the bigger picture.
In short, we live life as if it is the greatest emergency! We are always in a hurry solving issues, thinking of them as big problems and tend to occupy ourselves unnecessarily in small stuff, compounding them.

In the end, sweating the small stuff makes us lose precious times in our life.
After some time we begin to accept this as everything seems very hard and impossible - we ourselves invite depression.

We fail to recognize that the way we relate to our problems has lot to do with how quickly and how more efficiently we can actually solve them.
Learn the habit of discovering the remedies for your problems zone instead of fretting over them again and again.
When you learn to react more efficiently and respond to life with more ease, problems that seemed insurmountable will be more manageable.

An abundance of willpower and discipline are the key ingredients to eliminate most the hurdles of life. No hurdle is too high for us to overcome if we just believe in ourselves first. Your determination and positive thinking allows you to deal with the events of life more profoundly.

Presumably, there are other ways to relate to unexplained circumstances in life- a much more graceful approach when the path becomes easier to walk. The other way is to replace old habits of unnecessary reactions with all new habits of a change in perspectives. These new habits will help us to redeem more sustainable accreditations of life in true meaning of Living a more meaningful life.

I learn everyday and feel that I have still a lot to learn. Change the things that we can and accept what we can't. This simple strategy throws up new avenues. When we learn to let go
of problems instead of resisting them,and take them as challenges instead, life begin to flow one more time at ease and peace.

Routinely perform simple acts of kindness by being more patient even when everything around is in turbulence and you will be able to tackle all the odds of life.

This builds your inner strength making you accept life as it comes.

32. Pearls of Wisdom - Earth

The simple act of training your mind to be patient makes you more determined.

In life; *struggles ~ failures ~ problems ~ are all sometimes lined up...*

Keep your mind always prepared to overcome things with a simple strategy

I Can ~ I Will

Remind yourself that all problems are not going to last forever. This problems are to be taken as challenges, as lessons, to bring all your good qualities to the fore.

Take problems as being temporarily, with an absence of solutions at that particular time.
Change your entire perspective
into that of a creative master.
Foster the element of patience and be kind to yourself, rediscovering your original, unconditioned self. Develop patience, believe in yourself - you must

reclaim your brushes and start painting the canvas of life in vibrant colours.

Make problems your Stepping Stones reviving, you're Confidence One more time Just say, 'Yes I can'. Overcome what so over is on my way with ease.

So be patient, be grateful,walk courageously like the element earth.

Part B - My Journal

Precious Self

Precious self ~ divided into two segments categorised as:

1. Say •YES• to life
2. Yes I•CAN•

Make these affirmations a part of your life.

....Precious Life...

How much do we know ourselves?
It's important to understand yourself first how do we see ourselves.
The human brain is capable of being reflective.
It responds and is receptive. It can restrain many unacceptable thoughts. Precious self is to be aware of your own thoughts being speculative of circumstances preoccupied and being responsive accordingly

Saying yes to changes and accepting, adapting,re-focusing are the major influences on your mind-soul-body- life.
There's no challenge more challenging than the challenge to improve yourself. As light falls on the surface of any object, it can be reflected back or refracted. Similarly, situations, problems or hard times can be accepted or restrained.

Those who react to situations are impulsive and take decisions immediately without giving it a thought for

further impact. But those who are proactive are more responsible. They think and act accordingly, take time to analyse – visualise situations and further act to accept-adapt-change – as they know it's for their own growth enhancing their abilities,
polishing them, making them stronger to face all that's on the way of life.

I Say YES to Life

- I say Yes to live with a purpose
- I say Yes to live in today
- I say Yes to live in wellness
- I say Yes to live in positivity
- I say Yes to change my perceptions

1. I Say ~ YES to Live with a Purpose

Sometimes a tiny thought keeps reappearing, making me want to know more about my being here in this life.

Who am I? What's my purpose? Is my life with a purpose or just I'm here?

Looking back at my past, I was convinced that yes, I am here on a mission.

A mission filled with a true and positive purpose. No matter what our profession is, we are all here for some kind of purpose, is what my inner self reveals.

Home, luxuries, jobs, friend, relationships, money - these are mere attachments that we often mistake as our identity.

Discard your false identity. We are here to be in the service of mankind.

Every living individual is here with a purpose.

Every time you try helping someone else, you draw yourself closer to the purpose you're seeking.

Every time you try to listen to someone, you are closer to your purpose.

Every time you offer a simple help to the one who needs it, you are closer to your selfless service to the mankind,offering real meaning to being Human.

Your being there for someone may spark hope in their darkness of life.

That may be your purpose - start exploring who needs you.

To do good to someone or being kind does not cost you anything.

So add one more positive affirmative thought in your journal today.

Be a ray of sunshine in someone's cloudy, gloomy day. Spread smiles, spread kindness.

Remember everything will progress and work in the best way you would want only if you are ready for some hard work make some efforts towards your life make some sacrifices required to live the life more in positivity the life of your dreams it all starts with you and your purposeful living.

Say YES to living with a Purpose

Keep smiling. Keep shining

________________ Signature ________________date.

2. I say ~ YES to live in Today

Happy people shine brighter.

They create more spaces in life full of opportunities as they are able to focus their minds on growth and gain energy for purposeful living.
They live in today.
They follow schedules.
They nurture only thoughts which are positive and energetic.
They're not judgemental. While living in the present, they overcome all difficulties with great enthusiasm. They don't seek justification or clarification for things that are not working

They work on it to find a way out.

They know that the tremendous positive energy should not go to waste.

They have a true perception of the clear thoughts that keep them walking ahead of the crowd.

Sometimes it's necessary to stop participating in the problems.
It all begins with you.

If you care for yourself, you will be strong enough to care about all the other things in life.
Truly experience the depth of happiness daily in small achievements. This is true enlightenment. We can now erase all fears making heart filled in more life more vibrant and take up all positively, hence you can also make affirmations today to live in today.

Say ***YES to Live in Today.***

Living in today improving to know what went wrong how it can be rectified , so it does not occur again.

To manage a balanced life, you need to inculcate discipline and nurture some time management in your journal.

Write down the things to be done.

Prioritize your work according to the extent of what is most urgent or important. Try to figure out what you want to do first. If possible, do the most difficult task first.

Today will not be lasting.

Live in today like it is the best day of your life.

Let today be everything. Don't make
your present gloomy - be very clear.

Live in every moment. Look
at life as if it's only for today.
Enjoy your best, being in life. Let go of all worries.
As every moment passes, fill it more in enthusiasm,
cherish it with all you can

Bring that uniqueness in your life, know what you want.

Think of what inspires you the most. Be the master of what you can do more efficiently, with the craft of daily practice. Express your thoughts, feelings and just grab time to live in today.

Keep smiling. Keep shining.

_______________ Signature   ___________ date.

3. I Say YES to Living in Wellness.

Being cheerful, being at peace, being calm is always an extremely
significant way to enhance your mood and well-being.

The Stressed life, Poor eating habits and disturbed sleeping patterns are major daily stresses. Pressure to excel in your job or academics, owning the latest electronic devices... are all damaging to healthy living.

Stop Living Someone Else's Life.
Depression occurs when we wake up one day and realize that we are not living our own life. We are instead, trying to please our parents, our spouse, our children, or our friends.
Your life is yours; you are the sole scriptwriter of your life. Don't handover the key to happiness to someone else.

If at all you need to set boundaries, set some priorities - make a list of dos and don'ts.

Avoid negative influences. Write down negative thoughts. Write the positive ones now try to analyse the impact the negative thoughts make versus the positive ones thus now you make a better choice.

Writing down our thoughts and feelings can serve as an easy remedy.
We are uncomfortable expressing ourselves verbally. We feel less stressed out when we write our emotions on a page.

Spend some time enjoying the nature take your shoes off just feel the calmness of the green grass under your feet this relaxes you and makes you feel serene, Accomplish small pleasures in life they are the best ones acting as small packets of energy boosters.

Use positive affirmation. When you find yourself emotionally and physically fit, you start loving and living more, boosting your self-esteem.

You experience the joy of achievement in small accomplishments.
Care about how many people you can help than how much appreciation you receive.

Understanding that the excuses you make are nothing more than the fears.

Do what makes you really happy.
And remember: If something was hard to accomplish yesterday, it doesn't mean it will not be easy to do today.

Spend time in solitude daily. As this will take you more closer to yourself and that will make a drastic difference, you'll face the voices of disagreement though but still I insist being alone for some time with yourself works impeccably. Spending time alone will help you build your confidence. It will allow you to refuel the strengths that you need towards your vision for your goals.

Focus on living a healthy LIFESTYLE.

Include lots of vegetables and fruits in your diet in such a way that all the requirements of protein and vitamins are supplied to the body. Drink plenty of water to cleanse and regulate the body-water balance, also detoxifying the body. With all the fast processed life activities all our work stresses we have forgotten the laugh.

Daily laughter's boost you to a much higher levels of positive living. Laughter elevates your moods thus you feel more happy and make better decisions since you are more rich in positive thinking and wellness.

Be away from negative people who are just energy drainers just make a distance and adapt a healthy living.

Take time and view your life make the changes required The truth remains that there is only a thin line between making it happen and letting it happen so what are you deciding today, just make an affirmation today and say Yes to live in wellness.

Read good books.
Take a morning or evening walk.
Practice deep breathing.
Connect spiritually.
Breed positive thoughts.
And say yes to living in wellness, adding an element of self-care to living a more meaningful life.

Keep smiling. Keep shining.

________________ Signature ____________ date.

4. I Say ~ YES to Live in Positivity

Being positive is a very important element of Life. When we choose to be positive and stay strong, nothing can disturb our peace of mind and we overcome the dark fears. We inculcate the habit of activating the growth of success seamlessly.
Be positive and take on health, happiness, and prosperity
as major areas of change, accept it and work on it.

Promise yourself that no matter what you are facing right now, you will look at the brightest side of everything and make your optimism grow day by day, giving it the true meaning.
Your success depends on the strength of
your desires and the acceptance of positive thoughts - do all the rest simultaneously.

Prefer to choose positive words against all the negative connotations.

Even if you focus on a small goal - suppose you want to lose

weight, don't use words such as, "I am fat", or "I want to lose weight". These
are negative statements, bringing into the mind mental images of what you do not
want to receive. Just replace these with the positive words, "I am getting slim",
or "I have my ideal weight". Such words build positive images in your mind.
Affirm, using the present tense, not the future tense.

Muster hope even if you are in despair. Write down counter for every cause that keeps you worried about how to do the things and get the desired results more efficiently. Reject unnecessary negative assumptions. Recognize the cause of the negative and its impact and try to create good strategy. Fear, hate... are all interrelated. Try to rise above these energy drainers as soon as possible.
Distract yourself from all the negative things and the negative people. Learn to live today rather than regret the past in which you no longer dwell.

Tell yourself that 'Today is the best day of my life'. Reduce all unnecessary worries.

Continue the journey with only a positive note.

I Say Yes to LIVING IN POSITIVITY...

Keep smiling. Keep shining.

_____________ Signature _____________date.

5. I Say ~YES to Changing My Perception

Life is never easy.
Most influential people have cemented their legacies on failures.
Failure is a necessary part of life.
We should be wise and allow it to happen. With this positive note, make your journal proudly affirm the positive impact of failures such as...

'I say Yes to Changing my perception that Failures are setbacks.'

I choose to see it as:

1. ***An opportunity to grow.***
2. ***Recognise it as common.***
3. ***Everyone experiences it.***
4. ***I get a chance to take it as my responsibility.***

Just take it upon as to process upon all your weakness. It helps you access the 'let go' factor for the things or situations that you can't change.

Failures help you to go through pain - hence you connect to yourself to be learning more of your own selves.
Failures help you move ahead.
We often get many stories of hardships to share as inspiration.
Failures help you to forgive and seeds refined quality of being more in patience seeding you to the most strategic catch of life that is indeed let go move on.

When the right time arrives a butterfly must emerge a caterpillar cannot remain in its cocoon forever. Everyone should articulate a outline in terms of principles and philosophy for his or her own life.

You are the master of your destiny just remember this.

Begin to see your failures as blessings which opened the doors to the routes of self discovery.

Drive your life from within, search for the best the things that matters you the most, make priorities,yes now is the time to change your perceptions.

Keep smiling. Keep shining.

____________ Signature   _________ date.

Yes I • Can •

- Reconnect myself to me
- Handle difficult people ~situations
- Walk an extra mile
- Be Kind to myself
- Accept imperfections

1. Yes, I Can Reconnect to My Life

~ Quit the habit of the words, 'I'll try.'
Replace it with the new word

I Can.

I'll try means I feel compelled to do and don't want to do it. A 'try' is nothing more than that.

Start by saying, 'Yes' to any help if offered rather than saying,'No thanks'.
Erase all the phrases that have negative connotations, like 'could have done' or even 'should have done'.

These are statements full of stress...
Say energetic statements like

I am ... I will... I can...

Words of advice

Never select options like 'I may fail'. Instead affirm it as 'I may learn something new'.

Don't underestimate yourself.
Be confident speak clear distinctly.

Find new ways and opportunities even in disappointment.

Remain firm – fight, don't give up
Use courage to walk confidently into the direction of your dreams.

When in hard times, don't worry. Ask yourself what you would achieve by being worried.

Write down your problems, try to sort out priorities seeking the best solutions.

Feel more optimistic - share your thoughts and recognize that pessimism is just a fear.

Distract yourself from destructive thoughts immediately. Challenge angry thoughts with positive outcomes.

Recognize and reconnect all the broken strings, increasing your self-esteem.

Believe in the purity of purpose.

Struggling times just need courage.

Diligently apply the strategies and you will be amazed to see that you are beginning to scale new heights of your own potential.

Dedicate yourself to transforming your inner self. Culture your discipline into whatever you're pursuing.

On achieving small victories will double your willpower.

The best way to reconnect with yourself is through meditation. Practice closing your eyes for five minutes every day, focusing on your breath, gazing into your inner compass for more clarity. Being in peace this initiates practice of being in patience too, the key to most of the trouble making issues in today's stressful life.

Keep smiling. Keep shining.

____________ Signature ____________ date.

2. *Yes, I Can Handle Difficult Situations*

You know you've made right decision when there's peace and calmness in your life.

Sometimes life is too hard too loud, to hear your inner voice.

Be quiet – the inner voice has all the answers. When you are immune to negative people who drain your energy, you choose to save positive energy for yourself.

I am ... I will... I can...

Words of advice

Communication should be as clear as possible to avoid misunderstanding and drama, which are energy-drainers.

Recognize people, things and places causes that irritated caused negatives drained your positive self-keep distance draw lines set priorities.

Sometimes it is better to seek and understand the opinions expressed in the communication - don't command or demean others.

Sometimes, to be calm is best thing in a difficult situation.

Try to accept the change if you can.

Once accepted, instead of fretting over the past, start making the small changes required.

Spend more time taking care of yourself - start with meditation.

Find ways to calm your anxiety and ride the wave of depression, know that it
eventually will pass.

When life changes, it becomes necessary to become aware that there are always many

Choices and options. Try to opt for a different way.

There may not be many choices available,or the choices we want, but there are always choices. Open your mind, start thinking about all the positive results now. No matter how tiny the results are, look around, and you'll find more options.

Being optimistic is one of the best choices than all the other choices available now track the much obvious choice that many unknowingly opt is being in depression, just look at what puts in front of you, when you choose the better and more positive options.

Accept and face the fact that on the whole, life is treating you well.

Keep smiling. Keep shining.

____________ Signature ____________ date.

3. Yes, I Can ~ Walk Extra Mile

There's no limits to your dreams if you are looking for excellence - motivation is the fuel you need.
When you inculcate a little patience, you look forward to going an extra mile.
Say yes to walking a little more, taking the positive feedback that seeds the growth of prosperity. Seek advice, smile and step ahead motivate no matter how hard, you can be sure
everybody walks Say Yes I Can too and be prepared to walk that
important extra mile.

Words of advice

We all want to be part of a success. We know that the path is not smooth but we have to be on the road, walking.

The volume and the growth of your success is measured by the direction and enthusiasm
of your movements, the passion with which you move towards walk of life and how your success may

inspire others too and this attitude to walk an extra mile makes an influence in the journey.

Excellence is to keep beating past your own limitations and expanding at your edges. Practising more a little every day.

If you don't have a standard for yourself, you have no records to beat; and
if you don't have any record to beat, you can't excel.

What is your recent strategy towards working on your goals?

Explore it, redefine it, strive a little harder, going an extra mile. It makes you sharper and helps you excel in your abilities. Your potential expands to scale new heights of success.

Remember Going an Extra mile is an attitude and You will have to walk alone in that extra mile, but each step is to be embraced and honoured while keeping an eye on the destination.

Keep smiling. Keep shining.

__________Signature   __________date.

4. Yes, I Can ~ be Kind to Myself

When something doesn't work, it's only a sign that something much more is to be explored. The delays hardships are just the process of inculcating the key element that is patience.

If I'm thirsty for the glass of lime juice, I won't say, "Try get me lime juice". I would rather make an effort to get it for myself or would place an order for it. But I can't respond to the need of my body-brain saying, "I'm trying". Unless you quit the conditioned habit of saying, "I'm trying", you will never achieve your goals.

Words of advice

Brain and body coordinate in accordance to your urges. Brain commands body creates circumstances work hence done it's all correlated. So conditioning positive affirmative thoughts like; I can,

Settles all...

Very little is needed to find happiness by being kind to the self.
Being impulsive does not work.
Just seek random moments
To show that you care, that you love that you respect...

Be peaceful even when everything around you is unsettled and all went wrong
Make peace with imperfections
Try to restore all the broken strings...

Hope and faith makes it all work.

Never forget who you are.

No matter if you are hurt and broken, and even if that someone takes all from you but watch that broken of you that will make you strong just be kind to self.

Being kind, you become stronger and can conquer all.

It's important to recognize our individual growth.
We can fortify ourselves with our positive qualities, improve our strengths make ourselves shine in and out in happiness.

At every step, we have to accept the Real Challenges.

When you are immune to the opinions and actions of your circumstances or people, you won't be disappointed and will not be the victim of

unnecessary suffering. We can't live in Illusions - we need to know ourselves first- we need to know how much we are capable of...You have to lose yourself sometimes to see what you are
Just stop making assumptions.

The Best Stories Come From All the Struggles We Face on our Way towards Reaching Our Dreams. Some times Are odd very Indecisive But just believe in yourself and Remind yourself

'I Can'

Use the power of your words indirections of truth and love.

Keep smiling. Keep shining.

__________Signature __________ date.

5. Yes, I can ~ Accept Imperfections

It's human tendency to fit into life,even if it's like the proverbial round peg in a square hole.

We keep worrying so much about what people will think or hoping that we will be liked, having no real of our own self. The most important key is that no matter how much we always seek perfection around it comes only in the time we get only how much we can handle.

The most sufferings are prefixed to what we see things should be and how the things are been there precisely the difference is only in imagination and perception. All cannot be perfect. Accept as it is and work hard to suit you the best,

From friends to co-workers, to dates or relationships, people always trying to please everyone else, but do not give a thought to the self.

Words of advice

Accept imperfect things and situations. Work on it to make it perfect.

Expecting perfection from others is an act of arrogance.

If you are expecting perfection from others, you are indirectly trying to change them for yourself and trying to fit them in your frame.

Say yes to all the imperfections around you.

Don't relive the disappointment every time you don't get results - just give everyone fair chance.

Try to understand others and try to understand their circumstances, their life's ups downs... there can be many factors that explain the imperfections.

Like you accept beautiful fairy tales, try to accept all, everything, everyone as they are, where they are.

Acknowledge the levels of the efforts they make, to make things work. Trust that however hard it is being surrounded by imperfections, it is best to keep walking in the darkness until light appears.

One of the best successful positive element is that your thoughts make your world so do feed good ones.

Keep your eyes and mind open to accept the things that you can't change. Change the things you can't accept and just move on.

Keep smiling. Keep shining.

____________Signature ____________ date.

Part C - Rendezvous' Reflection Life A Candid Meet ......

RENDEZVOUS Reflections
Life, a Candid meet

"A thought so splendid:

A thought full of praise, I am your spelling of meaningful phrase –

Engaged in you meet me Candid- for I have a Say: Meet me I'm your Life'

What is the simplest strategy that works in turbulence

I'm in process to direct your stay more genuine making objectives shine in clarity.

What if I read you a simple quote starting with 'once upon a time '

And suddenly you realize that it was your story

of life time when every letter did I say met you in your closest realm.

Would you hear more or make my voice low As it would be brushed across each highs and lows

Would you need strength to hold the truth that

may say about the world you are in today

Or would you retrospectively

Change your Perceptions of life

Would you view it in other side of reflections...

You walked on fire leaving ashes behind

All your footprints just their remind

That you were trying to find

You struggled to make Thousands of your dreams

You begged for rain But there were no clouds sometimes...

Life uncovered unexplained events sometimes

made you break at points but you stood in solitudes at times...

Steps scorched on earth As you walked too long in sun that was the day you were there...

Searching the reflections that you thought were at nearby end...

Things you thought would define you, but pages were left blank at times...

Courage broke you in pains but you still kept the walk.....

In reminiscences though

Let me today reveal

One more side of your faithful flow...

There's another side of grief

Where memories bring smiles

Not just pains engulfed in Sorrows

Redirect your struggles as your stepping stones get

renovate your path like blessing your own soul...

Joy and peace are still there Sunlight is like on ripened grain

Gentle autumn's still to rain

I am still with you

In each new dawn

Step out of darkness stand in light. Just because you can't see

Does not mean god is so rude

Replenish your search

In serenity of life....

Truth is still that you have crossed all phases of pain..

Smile is still the crown on the frame. And be proud to read

You won the Storms of life Believe that God has you In his Arms

And your life is all in his Frame....

Keep Smiling
Keep Shining
Keep LIVING
For life is Awesome

Inderjit Kaur